S P I N D R I F T

STELLA GOODFELLOW

VANTAGE PRESS
New York

My thoughts are vibrant as the spindrift spray
Tossed through the air by errant winds.

FIRST EDITION

Published by Vantage Press, Inc.
516 West 34th Street, New York, New York 10001

Manufactured in the United States of America
ISBN: 0-533-09183-7

Library of Congress Catalog Card No.: 90-93302

1 2 3 4 5 6 7 8 9 0

Contents

SPINDRIFT

Time and Time Again

Time rushes on, and we rush with it,
And there's very little time in this busy life, to live it.
We should make time to rest awhile,
To listen to friends and remember to smile,
To stop—really stop—and let the world keep turning,
Go where it will, while we keep still;

Caring for animals, appreciating flowers,
Enjoying to the full this beautiful world of ours,
Feeling the sun, the rain, the wind,
In a slower, gentler state of mind.

Have you ever seen animals rushing
Except when driven by man?
No, they take their time and enjoy the peace
Whenever they can.

I am tired of life's busy trappings
And the noise and speed of cars,
The rush and tumble and wear and tear
That seem to go with us everywhere.

So today is the day, I'm happy to say,
When my world slows down on its merry way
And I have time and time again
For quietness, contentment, and love.

Newborn Love

Newborn love comes on fragile wings,
Dependent on eyes and touching hands,
Gossamer dreams, and those small things
Each lover knows and understands.

"No lovers were ever like this," they sigh,
"We feel just like singing and dancing all day;
But our hearts must grasp love while we're young," they
     cry,
"For with age it will wither and die away."

But this I will swear: when your bright youth goes,
And the years grow shorter and your body slows,
It is then love glows like a beacon fire,
With a heart of compassion, and true desire.

The Nun

Small black nun in the noisy bus,
I wonder what you think of us;
The drunken farmer mouthing vague obscenities;
The objectionable children sucking wet, smelly oranges,
The two angry ladies with their voices shrill
And the dark-haired boy who looks so ill.

Once you looked up from the book you were reading
And I thought I saw on your small soft face—
Your unlined, smooth, faintly downy face—
The flicker of a smile for this human race.
I hope I saw a smile, for I can't help feeling
That you'd like to be a part of this wordly throng,
If your years of convent training
Hadn't taught that this was wrong.

What do you give to the world, small nun,
Sitting so quietly, bothering none?
Would it not be wiser if your Order taught
That unless you go where sinning is,
Your goodness here is profiting naught?
Anything can be pure in antiseptic solution,
But we all have to sin before we ask for absolution.

So, come out into our world, little sister,
You'll find it filled to the brim
With a sweet and bitter mixture.

Dusk

The sky is being painted by the sun,
This day's allotted span is almost gone,
Nothing now remains but dusk
And thoughts of you, and Evensong.

What Do I Want?

Today in the town I heard a bird.
In the madness of Bloor Street a bird was singing.
Above the noise and stench of cars,
He rejoiced in the sun, remembered the stars
And sang to the world of his love of living.

And I saw the people hurrying by,
Frowning, too harried to hear his cry;
And I thought how simple his wants are, here:
Sky space to fly in, and freedom from fear.

Then I thought of the few things I want from life:
A loving heart to quieten strife,
Clear eyes to see the world around,
Listening ears when trouble is found.

Two gentle hands to help when I can,
Understanding, compassion for my fellow man,
My husband to love me, my children to care,
No violence toward living things, anywhere.

Time to sit back and reflect on life,
To be a good mother, good neighbour, good wife.

Haiku—1

Truth

Deep in the forest
The animals are anxious;
Man, the beast, has come.

Happiness

Paws touch ground, no sound;
Chelsea, the cat, is now here;
Life is one big Purr.

Beware

Owl's eyes boldly stare,
Search for movement everywhere;
Small creatures—take care.

H'm?

The flowers worry,
They turn in all directions;
Why are the bees late?

Comment

In the wee small hours of New Year's Day
The churches were open for people to pray;
The welcoming doors were lighted and wide,
But people were passing, not kneeling inside.

"The church holds nothing for us," they said,
"Or haven't you heard that God is dead?
Don't talk to us of your God of love
Who lives in an imaginary heaven above.

"All life is progression, and we have come too far
To believe in that beckoning, mystic star,
Which led to the humble stable, bare,
In fact, we can prove that it wasn't there.

"So close the door on unheeded prayer
And follow us to the new Messiah,
Who sends his disciples through boundless space
To reach the moon—not to touch God's face."

They sense no Creator behind star-studded skies;
They have souls of computers and radar eyes.
Searching only for truth, half-truths tremble before us,
While infinity clamours, in silent chorus.

Homeward

Where the wild waves roar and break
And foam crests swell in a mounting riot,
The seagull floats on the evening tide,
Lonely, remote, and quiet.

Far away, on a rock face, nesting,
The seagull's mate is calling, calling,
So with a thrusting upward striving
Of lovely white wings wildly beating,
With plaintive cries,
Westward he flies.

Dipping, swooping, rising, falling,
Gliding, plunging, wildly calling,
Beating against the wayward wind
Blowing fiercely above the foam,
Heavy wings surging, body urging,
The lonely seagull
Is flying home.

Flowers

I think the loveliest sounds I know
Are the lilting names of the flowers that grow
In garden and field, hedgerow and dell,
Like candytuft, celandine, and pimpernel.

Sundew and meadowrue,
Bouncing Bette and mignonette,
Tansy and pansy,
Anemone and rose;
Corn cockle and honeysuckle,
Phlox, box, and goldilocks,
Jack-by-the-hedge and saxifrage
And furry pussytoes.

Names of flowers ring along
Like Canterbury Bells and campion,
Foxglove and primrose,
Bluebell and lime;
Periwinkle, snowdrop,
Marigold, forget-me-not,
Angelica and goldenrod,
Violet and thyme.

Lavender, acacia,
Love-in-a-mist, magnolia;
Names of flowers are perfumed stories,
Lilies of the valley and morning glories.

Ship Shapes

Speaking of ships
With the stern on the left,
Or is it the right?
Or is that at night?
The bow I know,
But where is the poop?
And how do you tell
A ketch from a sloop?
How wet is a bilge?
How loud is a boom?
What keeps the mast up?
And where's the bathroom?

And one thing more—
When I've really sailed enough,
Which is the quickest way
To get off!

The Blessing

The preacher stood by the open door
Of the pretty village church
On a sunny morning in early May;
The floor was strewn with fresh clean straw
And sweet-smelling hay,
For this was a very special day.

Along the lanes from the cottages and farms,
Children came carrying pets in their arms;
Some were walking with woolly lambs and soft-eyed
        calves,
A donkey, some dogs, and a little tame fawn
And a billy goat with a crumpled horn.
They were coming to the church at the preacher's behest,
To be blessed.

The bells were ringing and the congregation singing
As the animals came through the door;
They walked up the aisles, and the people were all smiles
While the animals waited patiently on the straw.
From a hole in the wall, two little mice came running out
To see what the meeting was all about;
They gazed at the preacher who smiled at them gently,
So, curling tails round their toes, they listened intently.

"We are here," said the preacher, very solemnly to the
        animals,
"Because God loves you very much;
He wants His blessing to fall upon you,
He wants to give you His loving touch."

The animals listened solemnly,
They tried to understand
That all God's creatures, great and small,
Were safely held in His loving hand.

"And now God's blessing on you all," said the preacher,
"Let us pray: May love and happiness surround you,
May you receive only kindness the live-long day."
The animals slowly bowed their heads
Then quietly turned away,
Back to their cottages and farms,
But in a happy different way
Because now they knew they were beloved by God,
On this very special day.

Haiku—2

Daydreams

My thoughts are long thoughts—
Boundless skies, unchartered seas;
I'll need you with me.

Surprise

Daybreak is dawning;
It gave no warning to Night
Who is still asleep.

Guilt

No young oak trees here
And, cheeks bulging with acorns,
The squirrels know why.

House Guest

If you have a house
Inhabited by a mouse,
Please let it go free.

Hearts by the Busload

"The school bus is here, they're home!" I said
And hurried off to cut homemade bread
And fill the slices with cheese and meat
And all the things you like to eat,
A glass of milk, a cake or two—
And then I turned to look at you,
Standing alone on the sun-drenched grass.

I saw your face with its look of loss
And although not a single word was said,
I longed to give you more than bread;
To lay my hands on your dark brown head
And tell you, "Son, all this will pass,
Young hearts are brittle and they break like glass."

But your dark eyes looked through me
Like a young wary bird,
Pleading, "Mother, please, no questions,"
So I didn't say a word.
I'm a generation older
And my advice is seldom heard.

They talk about children by the busload, now
As they talk about a load of hay or bags of meal,
But every mother in her heart knows how
Her child is different, and she can feel
When he is troubled and when he is glad.
She can read in his face the kind of day he's had,
And she knows to her sorrow, when young hearts break,
You can't solve the problem with chocolate cake.

Imagine!

The lion and the unicorn loved to fight and play,
They were fond of one another in a special kind of way.
Lion lived in a cosy cave by the side of a curving stream,
Unicorn lived in a bluebell wood where he liked to lie and
    dream.

Each morning as the sun arose, they'd gallop to meet for
    fun,
Wide awake and ready to play, and laugh and fight and
    run;
But on this morning the lion was quiet,
He didn't smile, he didn't play,
"Let's go to the river to drink," he said.
"It's very hot today."

Lion walked to the river, his shadow right behind;
Unicorn followed after, but no shadow could he find.
"Look," said the lion, "in the water,
That is my face you can see;
I am so very handsome
And he looks exactly like me.
My mane is soft and curly
And my eyes are big and brown.
Now, come and see yourself in the water,
Come closer and kneel down."

The unicorn came closer and gazed into the water;
There was lion's mane, curly and free,
But a unicorn's face he could not see.
Lion looked at Unicorn and tried hard to be kind:
"That's because you don't exist," he said,
"You're only in my mind."

"Of course I exist," laughed the unicorn,
"Look at my mane, and hoofs and tail.
I'm as real as you, I'm a unicorn!
With a beautiful coat and a magical horn,
I even remember the day I was born!"
"No, no," said the lion, "that isn't true;
In all the world there is only you.
But you're a magical unicorn—now that is true!"

The unicorn walked slowly away,
His tail hung down, his face was sad.
"Goodbye, dear lion," he said through his tears,
"Thank you for all the good times we've had."
But lion ran after his friend and said,
"I don't really mind if you're just in my head;
To me you are real, and I just want to play
And to run and to fight in the same old way."

So, if you have never seen a unicorn,
Find a cosy cave by a curving stream
And a bluebell wood on a windy hill,
And if this story isn't all a dream
The lion and the unicorn will be there still.

Unspoken

Sometimes my thoughts burst into words
Which dance on the air, and sing with the birds.

And sometimes, just sometimes, the words may be there,
But they're muffled and sad, and fade in the air;

These are the words that should never be said, never read;
In the heart let them lie—unspoken.

Listen, Lord

I can look back on my life
And see all the mistakes I've gone and made,
How I've quarrelled with my wife
Or used my hand when I should have stayed.

I've lost my temper over some small thing,
Got all het-up over some mess I was in;
Said something mean to a real good friend
Or refused to help when it was easy to lend.

I've told a lie over something small
When it would have been kinder to say nothing at all;
I've repeated a confidence, remembered a wrong,
Passed by when I was needed, acted weak when I could
        have been strong.

But please forgive my lapses, Lord,
I'm just one weak old human being;
Guess I'm wrong most of the time
But this I'll never be a-seeing,

Because I'm stubborn, too, and proud;
Instead of forgiving foe and friend,
I carry malice to the end,
Yet if I'm wronged I shout it loud.

So when our time is come to meet,
Will you raise me to my feet?
Please hold my hand, Lord, if you can
And forgive this miserable, bad old man.

Weeds

I scattered the seeds upon the ground
And watched them grow in glad array.
Others watched too and said with disdain,
"Some of those are weeds,
They'll spread in the rain,
So pull them up and throw them away,
Don't let them live another day!"

I looked at the weeds with their yellow flowers,
Drinking in the sunny hours,
And I watered them to help them grow.
The garden flowers still grew up tall,
They didn't seem to mind at all
The dandelions that grew all round
In their ground.

Some of us are weeds and some of us are flowers,
But we all enjoy the sunny hours.
And then, of course, for all we know,
A baby weed into a rose may grow.

September

The night is alight with a myriad stars,
The harvest moon is riding high,
The birds are all sleeping, and silent their voices,
And lonely am I.

Divinity

Divinity, the cat,
Was very fastidious;
She wouldn't look at rats,
She thought they were hideous.
But on the other hand,
She wouldn't catch mice
Because she felt they were rather nice.
Her feeling for birds
She couldn't put into words,
But when she could get 'em,
She 'et em!

Why?

"Why are we here?" the young man said.
"Why, to love and be happy, whatever's ahead.
All life is a joke—gather flowers while you can,
You're entitled to take, when you're a young man."

"Oh, no!" said the girl, "life is not so cruel;
It is kindness and gentleness and the Golden Rule.
You do not take love—you give from the heart
To that special someone from whom you never
will part."

"Stuff and nonsense," said the old man, "real life is hard
    work,
And worry and debt, and no time to shirk.
You labour and worry, then sicken and die;
You struggle through life, and die wondering why."

"Oh, no!" said the old lady, "to live is to love;
To care for your family, and thank God above
For the blessings He's sent you, for husband and home,
Your wonderful babies—now with homes of their own;
For your garden and pets, and neighbours so kind;
For the love that surrounds you, and for your peace of
    mind."

Reason Enough

Scientists tell us of Saturn's rings
And that planet Mars doesn't have such things;
Although we see only one moon in place,
There are really many moons circling in space.

Little black holes, and acid rain,
The greenhouse effect is in the news again.
They tell the reason for the stars in the sky,
But I really don't want to know why.

I want to gaze at the stars at night
And wonder at their sparkling light;
After April showers to see a rainbow there
With magical colouring, rich and rare;

To marvel at the silver moon
And feel the warming of the sun,
To appreciate everything God has done,
Creating this beauty in the heavens above,
To watch over us with love.

Haiku—3

Reliance

When the troubles came,
Fairweather friends were all gone,
But you stayed by me.

Flood

Aspen trees quiver
By the rain-swollen river;
Grey water rat sighs.

Reaction

As the tide recedes,
Clams exposed, dig in with toes,
Show fear, disappear.

Appetite

Male praying mantis
Has no memories of sex;
She eats him, during.

The Loon

Far across the lake a loon is calling;
Lonely, so lonely.

Softly and silently snowflakes are falling;
Lonely, so lonely.

The water is cold and the wind blows keen,
For this calling bird that I have never seen
But only heard.

I send you my love, you haunting loon,
Crying so plaintively beneath the moon,
And sounding so lonely, so lonely.

Favourites

I love God's small creatures
And here is a rhyme
To tell what I've loved in my time:

Black furry squirrels with tails so fine,
Waddling ducks all walking in line,
Fat little rabbits with powder-puff tails,
Mischievous field mice, and large barnyard owls
Who are certainly cruel and ready to assault,
But it isn't their fault.

Cheeky little sparrows and budgerigars talking,
Chubby soft kittens forever stalking
Imaginary prey in curtains and grasses,
Pouncing on nothing, when it passes.

I love small donkeys by the sea,
And seagulls flying, white, and free;
House mice—well, they're rather sweet
And really, they only want something to eat.

I've loved to see butterflies enjoying flowers
And birds singing in gentle spring showers;
I've brought up many puppies
And I've loved them all, it's true,
But most of all, and best of all,
I've loved you.

Household Gods

Mrs. Clansonby, fashionable, smart,
Trained to perfection her housewife's art;
She used Mrs. Beeton's cookery guide
And invited her neighbours to visit, with pride.

Her house was bright and always gleaming
And her copper kettle happily steaming,
And when she opened wide her doors,
Visitors were dazzled by her floors.

She entertained with so much grace,
Her home was a quiet and peaceful place;
To her guests she was always quite disarming
And they left for home thinking, "Isn't she charming."

But Mrs. Clansonby, hostess, kind,
Became a person of another mind
When her children came home tired from school:
"Go straight upstairs!" was her golden rule.

"Don't let me hear you make a noise;
I can't stand the sight of you grubby boys;
Don't mark my floors, or the strap I'll take,
And no! You can't have a piece of cake."

Poor Mrs. Clansonby, socially giving,
Completely missed the point of living.

A Student's Prayer

Here comes the dawn, Lord, and a brand new day,
Help me to live it in Your own way;
Let me be kind to my fellowman,
Helping in every way I can.
May I never be so proud
That I can't mingle with the crowd;
Teach me humility—but not too much—
We all have to keep the common touch.

I hope You realise we all do our best
To pass Your strict 'no sinning' test,
But if we fall by the wayside, Lord,
I think we should be forgiven
Because we're students in this wicked world,
Just learning how to get to heaven.

So keep Your sense of humour, Lord,
With Your angels at heaven's portal,
And when we seem to fail You most,
Please remember we're only mortal.

Spoiled Rotten

If loving me with tenderness
And listening to my woe,
And sharing my joys and sorrows
For forty-six years or so;

If making me feel beautiful
By saying so, out loud,
And smiling at me everywhere,
Alone, or in a crowd;

If loving me in spite of,
Not because of what I am,
Means I'm spoiled rotten,
Well, I am.

Prayer

Tall spires rise from the churches,
Pointing to the sky,
Carrying prayers from people
To God on high.

Tall chimneys rise from factories,
Pointing in the air,
Carrying deadly poison
To God knows where.

Our chemicals stain the waters
And our acids choke the trees,
Our garbage kills the soil
And rancid oil fouls the seas.

We have sacrificed our birthright
To power, lust, and greed;
We have robbed this world of its beauty
To gain luxuries we don't need.

God, forgive us our trespassing,
Turn our thoughts from destruction so great;
Teach us how to heal the world's sickness
Before it's too late.

Benison

Daisy-fresh morning
And the flowers, yawning,
Open their petals to feel the sun.
Trees, in the shadows,
Stretch forth their branches;
See the small insects from their crevices run,
For they are just as anxious to begin the day
As all living creatures are, to work and play,
With the sun as a welcome benison.

In Memoriam

When I felt weak, you made me strong;
You were my wings when the way was long.
I still hear your voice in the calling wind,
See your encouraging smile in the golden sun;
And when I feel your touch in the gentle rain,
I know, full well, we shall meet again.

Gentle Ben

I remember gentle Ben,
He used to pull the baker's van;
They trotted briskly up the street
And Ben would proudly lift his feet.

He wore a straw hat on his head,
With a hole each side for his ears;
He always wore it in the sun
Until his daily work was done.
His bright red reins gave a jiggle with his sway
And the bells on his halter rang out gaily all the way.

Then they'd decide to stop awhile
And the baker would whistle, and Ben would smile;
It was then that I brought out my apple for him
And his lips brushed my hand with a gentle touch;
I loved him very much.

The van was white and very clean
With bread and cakes on every shelf,
And the possessive way Ben pulled that van
You'd think he baked them all himself.

I sometimes think I hear him trotting
Up the street, and stopping, smiling;
Gentle Ben was dappled grey,
I wish that he were here today
Because I loved him.

The Village Green

The village green is a sunlit meadow
    Where oxlips and buttercups and daisies grow,
There, a stream runs through,
    With a splash of sunny gleams,
And the village lads and lasses
    Stroll and dream their youthful dreams.

But the village street is shadowy
    On the way I go from school;
There, the oak trees spread their lovely arms
    And keep the pathways cool,
And the blossoms on the fruit trees
    Throw down shadows, just like lace,
While the antic wind sends showers of petals
    Down upon my face,
Till the sun is almost hidden,
    And the village in the shade
Is a quiet sheltered haven
    Like a secret forest glade.

Emergency

I've come to pray again, Lord,
Because we're really in despair;
We lost our fifteenth game today,
We're losing everywhere,
And I'm sure it would make a difference
If You were there.

I know it isn't whether you win or lose
But how you play the game,
Yet however sportsmanlike we are,
We're losing just the same.

Thank you, Lord, for listening,
As I'm sure You always do,
And I know You'll be there at the playing field
Tomorrow at half-past two.

Harvest

"You only reap what you sow, you know,"
The farmer said with pride;
"The very best seeds that I could find
Went into those fields, and look at them now,
That wheat is veritable treasure,"
And he slapped his thigh, for good measure.

I think to reap what we sow is fair,
And I planned to sow my seeds around,
Of kindness, courtesy, and love;
And then, if they're fair in heaven above,
And all my promises I keep,
What a wealth of happiness I shall reap.

House Rules

"There's just one more thing," the landlord said,
"Please don't feed the pigeons, they're dirty things.
They darken the balconies and make a noise with their
    wings;
They shriek when they're hungry, and coo when they
    wake.
So leave them alone, for goodness sake!"

I thought about what he had said, when he'd gone,
But not for long.
I looked from my balcony and I saw
Pigeons and sparrows and seagulls galore,
With white wings like angels and orange webbed feet,
And they all stood there waiting for something to eat.

I threw them some bread and a muffin or two
And watched them all scramble—as hungry birds do;
So it gave me great pleasure to throw them some more,
But nevertheless I have to confess,
They did make a mess on my balcony floor.

"My Goodness!"

There's a chair in our house
Which isn't made of wood;
It's full of deep soft cushions,
And when I'm very good
And promise not to squiggle
Or squirm, or roll around,
I'm allowed to sit upon it,
But I mustn't make a sound.
So I sit up tall and straight
And I smile a little smile,
And I'm very, very good
For a very little while.

Good Stuff

This is the stuff that dreams are made of:
Toadstools, mushrooms, and leprechauns,
Dandelion parachutes, and unicorns,
Bird songs and madrigals
And moonlight nights.

This is the stuff that love is made of:
A listening heart and empathy,
Smiling eyes and courtesy,
Leading to passion and ecstasy;
This is the stuff of love.

We need our dreams and fantasies,
The thoughts and hopes that tomorrow brings,
And from all these fleeting yet tenuous things,
We find the wonder, the safety,
And the comfort of love.

Trees

It must be pleasant to be a tree,
To hold a nest of birds in the fork of a bough,
To provide cool shelter for horse and cow,
To stand by a pool and give your leaves, torn,
To the moose and the deer and the gentle fawn.

To feel warm sun and the falling rain
Make drooping twigs stand straight again;
To be tall in the spring, with your branches swept
By a wild March wind, and know you have kept
Your roots still firm in the good sweet earth,
Where the acorn first grew that gave you birth.

Strong, reaching trees must be Nature's pride,
Standing through the seasons, side by side;
Naked in winter, sleeping buds closed tightly,
Awakening in spring, new leaves shining brightly;
Changed by the magic of the season's fall
To flaming red and burnished gold, most beautiful of all.

Feed the Birds

The world is grey, and all around,
Small birds wait patiently on the ground,
With their feathers fluffed, one foot held high,
Small bodies feeble, too tired to fly.
The snow blows wild, and their cries are hurled
By the searing wind, to an unhearing world.

But when wintry sun melts the covering snow
And all the trees their blankets throw,
Fruits are uncovered and seeds abound;
All the birds chatter with a cheerful sound.
They forgive our neglect and fling forth a song
From a bundle of feathers and a heartbeat strong.

Haiku—4

Tally-ho

Big brave men in pink,
Horses, dogs, and ladies fair,
Tear the screaming fox.

Jaws

Wee bodies, legs, wings;
Bugs are the tiniest mites
With the largest bites.

Shepherd

Ripe with wild berries,
The hedgerows stand sentinel
Over green pastures.

Taste

They brought the nuts back;
"Thank you," said the squirrels, "but
We don't eat roasted!"

Replete

The crocodile lay on the banks of the Ness,
Smiling crocodile smiles through crocodile tears;
"I've eaten the Loch Ness monster," he bragged,
"I've been wanting to do it for years."

Home

Out of the bare rocks, the ugly tree
Thrust twisted and dark against the sky,
But thrushes liked its symmetry
And built their nest in its leafless branches.
I wonder why.

Grapevine

The black grapes grow more swollen
And hang heavier on the vine;
The grape leaves look astonished
And cling closer to the trellis.

Bard

"Your poems are never neat enough.
Why don't you write a sonnet
That we may feel the strength of it,
The rhythm and the rhyme of it?
Please try to write a sonnet."

But sonnets are like gardens
With flowers all in line,
Roses at attention,
Grapes, by numbers, on the vine.

I like my garden simple,
Flowers growing where they may,
With birds, bees and butterflies
Paying visits every day.

So that's why my poems are at variance,
Why my sentences normally appear
To have neither rhyme, rhythm nor reason;
After all, my name isn't Shakespeare.

With Gusto

When I arise at morning light
The moon and stars are out of sight.
The songbirds welcome the coming day
But the sky and the clouds are heavy and grey.
Perhaps the stars shouldn't hurry away
On such a wet and thundery day;
I'd like to see their twinkling smile
If they would only stay awhile.

But the rain clouds open and the rain falls down,
The wind is angry and he acts like a clown,
Tearing through the fields of ripening grain
And washing all the windows with cataracts of rain;
Impatient and sullen he hurries on,
Sweeping the clouds till the storm has gone
And the sky turns blue and the sun comes out—
And that's what weather is all about.